DO ANY OF THESE SOUND LIKE YO[U]

- [ ] You've ordered groceries for delivery to avoid the people at the store.

- [ ] You've pretended not to be home when your groceries were delivered.

- [ ] You've been concerned that a dog was judging you.

- [ ] You've been concerned that a cat was judging you (she was).

- [ ] You wanted to try yoga to de-stress but were worried you'd be bad at it and decided not to show up.

- [ ] You swap between different coffee places because you don't want the staff to start recognizing you.

- [ ] You agreed to meet your friend's new boyfriend, but instead you waited until the last minute and texted that you're leaving the country.

- [ ] You wo[rry]
you've [...]

- [ ] You worry that you're being a hypochondriac for worrying about the headaches you've been having.

- [ ] But what if you're not being a hypochondriac? You're worried about that, too.

- [ ] You're worried about offending spam callers by not picking up.

- [ ] When you hear a group of people laughing on TV, you assume it's about you.

- [ ] You have a game plan and an emergency kit for the zombie apocalypse, or if the corner store runs out of toilet paper.

- [ ] You've been irritable for so long that this is just who you are now.

- [ ] You're reading this list.

If you can relate to any of these scenarios, anxiety might have a grip on you. If you're tired of living this way, you've picked up the right book. Join me on an adventure of exploration and discovery in this *5-Minute Anxiety Relief Journal* to stop freaking out and start living fully.

THE
5-Minute
Anxiety
Relief
Journal

THE
5-Minute
Anxiety
Relief
Journal

A CREATIVE WAY TO STOP FREAKING OUT

Tanya J. Peterson, MS, NCC

Illustrations by James Olstein

ROCKRIDGE
PRESS

To all the strong
and resilient people out there
who aren't giving up the quest
for an anxiety-free, quality life.

You've got this!

This Journal Belongs to

_____

Interior and Cover Designer: Suzanne LaGasa
Art Manager: Janice Ackerman
Editor: Samantha Barbaro
Production Editor: Kurt Shulenberger
Custom Illustration: © 2019 James Olstein

ISBN: Print 978-1-64611-291-3

R0

CONTENTS

MACGYVER YOUR ANXIETY

Welcome to *The 5-Minute Anxiety Relief Journal*. You've just opened a book that will help you take away anxiety's power over your life so you can regain control. Anxiety has a way of making us feel like we're alone, the only ones who are plagued by worries, fears, and anxious thoughts. However, that is nothing more than one of anxiety's nasty little tricks to manipulate you. Check out the numbers that expose anxiety as a liar:

* In the United States, 40 million adults, or 20 percent of people, live with some type of anxiety disorder, as reported by the National Institute of Mental Health.

* Worldwide, 264 million people have an anxiety disorder, according to the World Health Organization (WHO).

* A whopping two-thirds of all people polled by the American Psychiatric Association in 2017 experienced anxiety but didn't meet the criteria for an anxiety disorder (such as length of time living with it, number of symptoms, and degree of life disruption).

You are not alone in your anxiety; in fact, you're in great company. You may have noticed that above I used the words "us" and "we." I did so intentionally because I used to struggle with anxiety, too, before I gathered up some important tools and committed to regaining my life. I'm sharing many of these tools with you here so you can do the same!

You already have what it takes within you. You can take bits and pieces of yourself, shape and form them, and create a powerful super tool, operated by you, to escape from and destroy your anxiety. You're basically MacGyver (in case you don't know or don't remember, he's that guy from the TV show who saves the world with a shoelace and little packets of ketchup).

Remember this fact as you move forward with this journal: Anxiety is treatable. No matter how much it has plagued you and controlled you, it isn't you. You aren't your anxiety! Therefore, you can move right along and leave it in the dust of the past.

Part of the process involves distancing yourself from your anxiety. Separating yourself from anxiety gives you space and wiggle room. You can begin to stretch and dance and feel unburdened. Try it now, just to see what it's like to move freely. Take a slow deep breath, reach up to the sky, wiggle your fingers, and then slowly bend forward as far as you can go; if you're as inflexible as I am, that probably won't be far, but who cares? Then stand and shake anxiety loose.

Still feel anxious? That's okay. You're about to embark on a journey that will empower you to take care of anxious thoughts. This journey will be fun. This book, while evidence based, is peppered with humor and levity. Anxiety is heavy. When you can smile and chuckle, you begin to distance yourself from it. You gain new perspectives and get out of your head. You stop freaking out.

Less Time Than It Takes to Warm Up a Hot Pocket

Think of this book as a friendly guide to help you maximize your existing tools and learn to activate new ones. As you work through *The 5-Minute Anxiety Relief Journal*, you'll find useful information about anxious thoughts and conquering anxiety. The power of the journal lies in applying this information to your own anxiety to shape the quality life you deserve to live.

Ideally, you'll work through this journal in order by chapter because it's progressive. You'll learn to recognize unhelpful thought patterns and take action to change and move past them. Enjoy the process as you create welcome relief.

Stress about time and tasks is a very common source of anxiety. If you experience this, know that this journal is designed to alleviate anxiety rather than pile on more. To that end, all the exercises are designed to be completed in about five minutes. They're short and sweet—and powerful.

You just might discover that you can do these exercises in less time than you'd spend making a Hot Pocket. True story: Once, pretending to get out of preparing lunch for my daughter, I listed the steps I'd need to take to make a Hot Pocket. I came up with 24. I really milked the process. My daughter didn't buy it, and I made the Hot Pocket. Not only was it much quicker and easier than I made it out to be, it ended up being fun with a positive result (one scalding Hot Pocket). That's what you'll find in this journal.

Turn the page, grab a favorite pen or pencil, and *Stop Freaking Out!*

"Like bad ice cream, there are many, many varieties of anxiety."

chapter one

KEEP YOUR FRIENDS CLOSE AND YOUR ENEMIES CLOSER: BUDDY UP TO YOUR ANXIETY

You're on your way to freedom from anxiety! As with any journey, it's important to know what you're dealing with so you don't get stuck. In this chapter, you'll find information and prompts that let you investigate your own unique anxiety. "Anxiety" is a broad term. No two people experience it the same way. What is your anxiety like? Maybe you constantly worry about many things, or you're anxious around people. Is your anxiety stress related? One thing is certain: Anxiety is nagging and plaguing. The prompts in this chapter will bring you close to your anxiety so you can observe and understand what it's like for you to live with it.

Like IKEA Furniture, Everyone Has Some

Everyone experiences some anxiety: It's hardwired into the human brain. Anxiety has been with humanity since the beginning. Long ago, if a distant ancestor was threatened, the brain instantly reacted with fear and automatically activated our fight, flight, or freeze system. Today, our threats are different, but they still exist. Navigating relationships, worrying about making ends meet, or even fretting about working time into your schedule for self-care, we still have anxiety: It's a defense mechanism.

Anxiety becomes a problem when it takes over and causes us to see threats where they don't exist. Our lives become overpowered by fear, worry, and the fight, flight, or freeze response. Once you recognize how anxiety affects you, you can start to create different responses.

More Terrible Flavors Than Baskin-Robbins

Anxiety comes in many terrible varieties—all worse than rum raisin ice cream (frozen raisins?). Everyone's variety of anxiety is different. Common types include:

* separation anxiety disorder (anxiety when you're not with a loved one)

* specific phobias (intense, irrational fears)

* social anxiety disorder (fear of being judged or embarrassed)

* panic disorder (seemingly random panic attacks)

* agoraphobia (fear of leaving the house)

* generalized anxiety disorder (excessive worry about many things)

* anxiety attacks (like panic attacks but occurring in response to worry or stress)

* stress-related anxiety (worry about one or more stressors in your life)

* existential anxiety (anxiety about your existence and where your life might go)

* performance anxiety (fear of failure in any part of your life)

Panic Attacks, Shaky Hands, Flushed Face, Upset Stomach . . .

Anxiety is everywhere: in our brain and in our body. When we're anxious, our brain commands the body to prepare to fight, flee, or freeze. Hormones like cortisol, adrenaline, and norepinephrine flood the body so the entire system can react. This creates physical misery, and can even cause these symptoms:

* chest pains that feel like a heart attack

* tense, sore muscles

* shaky hands

* headaches

* stomachaches or nausea

Anxiety's physical symptoms can mimic illnesses, including a heart attack. Too often, people end up with expensive medical bills from rushing to the ER, only to be sent home. The prompts in this book will help you take back your body.

You Have to Work Together, but You Don't Have to Like Each Other

Have you noticed that when I talk about anxiety, it's separate from you? Anxiety is "in" your brain and body. "It" has many varieties and causes physical symptoms in "your" body. That is because you are not your anxiety, and you can build a new life without anxiety hanging around. This will require you to spend some time working *with your anxiety.* When you know specifically what it's like and how it affects your thoughts, emotions, and behaviors, you'll gain insight into how you can replace anxiety with freedom and happiness.

Are you ready to dive in? Let's go!

"Start where you are. Use what you have. Do what you can."

—ARTHUR ASHE

If your idea of being anxious is too vague, you'll find it difficult to know where to focus your attention and how to begin. Uncover your details. When you think about having anxiety, what do you mean? Describe a recent day on which you had anxiety.

_____

_____

_____

_____

_____

_____

_____

_____

_____

_____

_____

Close your eyes, and tune in to your body. Starting with your feet and progressing slowly to the top of your head, identify where you hold anxiety. List all the places you feel anxiety. Rank them from most bothersome to least bothersome by numbering them, with number 1 representing the most bothersome.

_____

_____

_____

_____

_____

_____

_____

_____

_____

_____

_____

The fight, flight, or freeze response is a protective instinct. To fight means to stand up to a threat and push back. To flee is to avoid a problem. To freeze is to take no action. What response do you use more than the others? How does it work (or not work) for you?

_____

_____

_____

_____

_____

_____

_____

_____

_____

_____

_____

_____

Hating anxiety makes sense, but hating anxiety also strengthens it. That hate puts your focus on the anxiety rather than on freedom. To say goodbye to your hate it's important to make peace with it. On the top half of the page, draw a picture of yourself letting go of the hate. On the bottom half, draw yourself free from hatred.

Anxiety makes you see threats where there aren't any. Close your eyes and picture a person or situation that makes you agitated, concerned, fretful, or worried. List your anxious thoughts about this person or situation. Describe one thing that might be your anxiety thinking for you.

_____

_____

_____

_____

_____

_____

_____

_____

_____

_____

_____

_____

How are you today? People ask each other that a lot, often without thinking or even wanting an answer. I'm asking you that question, and I'm being intentional and sincere. How are you? Check in with yourself about how your anxiety is affecting you today, and then write your response.

_____

_____

_____

_____

_____

_____

"Knowing yourself is the beginning of all wisdom."

—ARISTOTLE

Archaeologists help us understand what human life was like in the past by finding artifacts, piecing them together, and seeing a bigger picture. Become an anxiety archaeologist. Uncover your anxiety and find its pieces within you. What random thoughts or emotions do you uncover? Do you feel physical tension or other sensations? Describe the details of the pieces of your anxiety you're uncovering. (For example, maybe you found gems like these: *My anxious thoughts are worse first thing in the morning. I worry about many different things every day. I worry only about money, but I worry a lot and can't stop thinking about it.*)

_____

_____

_____

_____

_____

_____

_____

_____

As your own anxiety archaeologist, you wrote about some of the anxiety you uncovered within yourself. Consider what picture of you these thoughts create. Describe this image of yourself based solely on these snippets of anxiety.

_____

_____

_____

_____

_____

_____

_____

_____

_____

_____

You are not your anxiety. Look back at what you wrote about yourself based only on those fragments of anxiety. It is probably very one-sided and inaccurate. Let's get more real. You aren't anxiety, so who are you? Put on your introspection helmet and once again go exploring. Describe or list some things that make you *you*.

_____

_____

_____

_____

_____

_____

_____

_____

_____

_____

What bothers you and negatively affects your life? Check all
that apply.

☐ fear

☐ stress

☐ worries

☐ panic attacks

☐ social fears or worries

☐ the nature and direction of your life

☐ failure

☐ overthinking

Now, narrow down your anxiety a bit more. Of the items you
checked, circle one or two that are the worst right now.

You just checked off types of anxiety that are limiting your life
more than others and circled what topped the list. Choose one
of your circled items and go deeper. How is this type of anxiety
affecting you and your ability to live the life you want and deserve?

_____

_____

_____

You're in an anatomy class, and you must give a presentation about where you experience anxiety in your body. (If even the make-believe scenario of giving a presentation increases your anxiety, I apologize! But you can use the feeling to respond to this prompt.) How does your body let you know that you have something to fear or worry about?

_____

_____

_____

_____

_____

_____

"I define anxiety as experiencing failure in advance."

—SETH GODIN,
POKE THE BOX

Anxiety is personal, and we all have our own definition of it. How do you define anxiety?

_____

_____

_____

_____

Words can have synonyms, or other words and phrases that have meanings similar to the original. Identifying some synonyms can help you better understand a word, especially one as complex as anxiety. If, for example, your anxiety involves a great deal of worry, what other words would you use to deepen the meaning of worry?

_____

_____

_____

_____

_____

Words can also have antonyms, or other words and phrases that have meanings opposite to the original. Look back at your definition of anxiety and your synonyms. What is the opposite of them? Your life without anxiety will be the opposite of life with it—what will that life be like?

_____

_____

_____

_____

_____

_____

_____

_____

_____

_____

If you are not your anxiety (and you most definitely are not), who are you? Design a T-shirt logo that proudly shows who you are when anxiety goes away. In times of self-doubt and anxiety, imagine yourself wearing the T-shirt and logo with pride.

Why that shirt? Do you ever wonder when you shop for clothing why you like what you do? You just designed a T-shirt. Why did you choose the words and/or images you did? Write about the meaning of your design.

_____

_____

_____

_____

_____

_____

_____

_____

_____

_____

_____

In what ways is your anxiety limiting your life? Knowing how you're being limited will help you know what you want to change. Think about relationships, activities, inner peace, physical wellness/illness—any areas that aren't as positive as you'd like them to be.

"Do one thing every day
that scares you."

—MARY SCHMICH,
CHICAGO TRIBUNE

If you were ordered to do one thing that scared you every day, could you do it? Assuming that you could (you're stronger than you realize), what are some things that you would do? What would it be like to begin? How would you feel every day after completing the feared action?

_____

_____

_____

_____

_____

_____

_____

_____

_____

_____

_____

_____

Knowing what your current anxiety is like helps you know what you're dealing with so you can approach it effectively. Similarly, knowing where you want to go gives you direction. What are your goals for your anxiety-free life?

_____

_____

_____

_____

_____

_____

_____

_____

_____

_____

Sometimes, anxiety isn't bothersome and can be ignored. What must happen in your life for anxiety to start bothering you? In other words, when does anxiety become a problem for you?

_____

_____

_____

_____

_____

_____

_____

_____

_____

_____

_____

_____

Taking short, five-minute breaks throughout the day to meditate helps calm your thoughts and emotions. Try this simple deep-breathing meditation to start your calming journey:

* Set a (gentle) alarm for five minutes.

* Close your eyes. Inhale slowly and deeply for five counts.

* Hold your breath for a few seconds.

* Exhale for seven counts, slowly and thoroughly.

* Repeat until the five minutes is up.

A day in your life: the morning. When you wake up in the morning, what's the first thing you notice? When do you first notice anxiety? How do you keep going despite your anxiety?

_____

_____

_____

_____

_____

A day in your life: the afternoon. Where are you, and what do you do on a typical afternoon? How is your anxiety compared to what it was in the morning?

_____

_____

_____

_____

_____

A day in your life: nighttime. How do you experience anxiety as you wind down your day? Does your anxiety keep you up at night? Describe how anxiety affects your sleep (or, if it doesn't, how you've taken charge of your sleep).

_____

_____

_____

_____

_____

_____

_____

_____

_____

_____

What makes you anxious? Brainstorm a list of people, places, activities, and other things that can cause your anxiety to spike. How do you feel when your anxiety skyrockets?

_____

_____

_____

_____

_____

_____

_____

_____

_____

_____

_____

"I'm here to talk to me about me. I have some complaints."

chapter two

NEGATIVE THOUGHTS: GET TO KNOW THE GROUCHY NEIGHBOR IN YOUR BRAIN

The brain is the only organ that can make itself anxious. With the instinctive need to scan for danger, along came a negativity bias and automatic negative thoughts (ANTs). The brain finds the negative much more quickly and easily than it does the positive, and that makes it a grouch. As a result, we often feel agitated, stressed, and anxious.

Some astonishing statistics about our ANTs:

* We have 50,000 to 80,000 thoughts per *day*.

* This means approximately 2,100 to 3,300 thoughts every *hour*.

* Of these, *70 percent* are negative.

If anxiety has ever made you feel like your head will explode, this might explain it! This chapter is all about the negativity bias, automatic negative thoughts, and the feelings that result. There's nothing negative about what you're about to discover and do!

You Don't Even Know You're Doing It

The human brain continually scans for problems, and it's very good at finding them. This search for problems happens automatically, without you realizing that it's happening. As a result, these negative thoughts are automatic. When they run amok, they cause significant anxiety.

You can locate your anthills and flush out the ANTs. As you progress through this chapter, you'll learn how to identify your ANTs, and you'll explore them to question their validity. Thoughts aren't true just because you think them—remember, anxious thoughts appear because of the negativity bias, not because they're real. Empower yourself by replacing automatic, negative, anxious thoughts with purposeful, positive, precise ones.

If Your Thoughts Were on Facebook, You Would Have Blocked Them by Now

Anxious thoughts are usually harsh, mean, judgmental, and untrue. They distort your reality, but they make you think they're accurate.

ANTs take specific forms. Some of the thought patterns to watch for, and block, are listed in the chart on page 31.

TYPE OF NEGATIVE THINKING	HOW IT CAUSES ANXIETY
Labeling	Makes you call yourself names (like "stupid" or "incompetent").
Jumping to Conclusions and Catastrophizing	Makes you assume things will go wrong or that you can't handle something.
Emotional Reasoning	Permits your feelings to determine your thoughts, such as thinking something is dangerous because you feel uneasy.
"Should" Statements	Imposes rigid rules on you, others, and life.
All-or-Nothing Thinking (aka Black-and-White Thinking)	Causes you to think in extremes and blinds you to everything in between those extremes.
Personalization	Makes you blame yourself (or others) for situations and doesn't let you see other possibilities.

Surprise! Keeping It All Inside Isn't Good for You

Many people don't want to deal with anxiety's harsh feelings, so they bottle them up. Ignoring these emotions is understandable, but it comes with dire consequences. Repressed feelings don't disappear. They can turn into physical symptoms like headaches, pain, fatigue, dizziness, and more. They can also hunker down and grow. They're basically like Gizmo from the movie *Gremlins*, and they'll eventually get wet and you might feed them after midnight. When that happens, look out. To avoid an explosion of evil gremlins and intensified anxious emotions, it's important to address your repressed feelings. This journal is a safe start. Be honest with yourself as you explore anxious thoughts and feelings.

Your Feelings Aren't Wrong, but They Do Cause Problems

Feelings simply are what they are. Your feelings are legitimate. They can also, however, be part of a vicious cycle that worsens anxiety. An ANT evokes a certain feeling, and when you experience the feeling, it reinforces the anxious thought. This, in turn, intensifies the feeling, which strengthens the anxious thought, and so on.

Taking control back from anxiety is ultimately about breaking the cycle of self-perpetuating thoughts and emotions. First, though, you have to understand your own negative thoughts. Let's get into some self-discovery!

> "It is our attitude at the beginning of a difficult task which, more than anything else, will affect its successful outcome."
>
> —WILLIAM JAMES

Let's begin with general awareness of your negative thoughts. Think of a recent time when you felt anxious, worried, and/or afraid. What were you thinking about the situation and yourself? Recall as many thoughts as you can. Has your anxiety increased right now, as you think about the situation?

_____

_____

_____

_____

_____

_____

_____

_____

_____

_____

Automatic negative thoughts lead to upsetting emotions. What is a negative thought you have about yourself? Write it down. This is a thought you have about yourself every day, sometimes consciously as a reaction to something, and other times subconsciously without fully realizing it. What feelings does this thought lead to?

_____

_____

_____

_____

_____

_____

_____

_____

_____

_____

_____

Thoughts begin simply enough, but the more they run through our minds, the bigger they grow until they become beliefs that we "know" are true. What is a belief you have that contributes to your anxiety? If you can, list more than one.

_____

_____

_____

_____

_____

_____

_____

_____

_____

_____

_____

Time for a pop quiz! Since this is for your own growth rather than proving your knowledge, you won't be graded. Match the ANT on the left with an example on the right. Oh, and it's okay to use your notes (as in the chart in this chapter on page 31).

ANTS	EXAMPLES
_____ "should" statements	1. If I don't get into this college, my life will be ruined. I'll end up working at fast-food restaurants forever.
_____ all-or-nothing thinking	2. Why do I let him walk all over me? I'm weak and spineless, that's why.
_____ labeling	3. I feel humiliated. Everyone is laughing at me because I dropped my sandwich. I can't handle a party like this, and I'm leaving. I'm done with them.
_____ personalization	4. I shouldn't have yelled at my son. His day will be ruined, and I've driven a wedge between us.
_____ emotional reasoning	5. My daughter's bike was stolen, and it was my fault for not buying her a better lock.
_____ catastrophizing	6. If I don't get this promotion, it means they don't value my work, and I'll be fired.

ANSWER KEY: 4, 6, 2, 5, 3, 1

ANTs aren't always straightforward. Some of them are similar to others, and usually thoughts are made up of more than one ANT. What ANTs are often at work for you?

_____

_____

_____

_____

_____

List some thoughts that are very bothersome to you. Look for patterns. What's going on when you have these thoughts? How do they affect your emotions and actions?

_____

_____

_____

_____

_____

_____

"The primary cause of unhappiness is never the situation but your thoughts about it. Be aware of the thoughts you are thinking. Separate them from the situation, which is always neutral, which always is as it is. There is the situation or the fact, and here are my thoughts about it. Instead of making up stories, stay with the facts."

—ECKHART TOLLE,
*A NEW EARTH: AWAKENING
TO YOUR LIFE'S PURPOSE*

What will it be like when you can be in a situation and let your thoughts about it go? How will your life be better?

_____

_____

_____

_____

_____

_____

_____

_____

_____

_____

_____

_____

When you separate a situation (which is neutral) from your thoughts about it (which are often negative and emotionally charged), it reduces anxiety and creates inner stillness. Reflect on the thoughts currently streaming through your mind. Pluck one and write it down. Then, add "I'm having the thought that" in front of it. Repeat several more times. Practice this often to learn the skill of distancing yourself from your thoughts.

"Should" statements impose strict rules on how you "should" or "should not" be and what you "should" or "should not" have done. What rules do you give yourself? How do they affect your anxiety levels?

_____

_____

_____

_____

_____

_____

_____

_____

_____

_____

_____

When we are anxious, our negative thoughts are in the past or in the future. "I Spy" is a mindfulness exercise to help you keep your thoughts in the present moment. You can sit where you are, or you can go for a mindful walk. Look around and note what you see, saying to yourself, "Right now, in this moment, I see . . ." Write these things down or draw them in the magnifying glass.

Does anxiety tell you you're not good enough? What, specifically, does it make you believe, and in what circumstances do you feel inadequate? Now, look for evidence that you are, in fact, good enough. What do you do well? What do you do that is "good enough," or even great?

_____

_____

_____

_____

_____

_____

_____

_____

_____

_____

List a few anxious, negative thoughts you tell yourself. Now, reword them to take away the negative, judgmental tone. For example: "What if I screw up? Everything will be ruined," can become, "I may do really well, or I may make a mistake. If I make a mistake, it won't be a disaster, and I can handle it."

_____

_____

_____

_____

_____

"Anxiety is a thin stream of fear trickling through the mind. If encouraged, it cuts a channel into which all other thoughts are drained."

—ARTHUR SOMERS ROCHE

When your negative thoughts are fewer and weaker and anxiety has lost its power, what will your thoughts be like instead? Describe them in detail.

_____

_____

_____

_____

_____

Getting in touch with feelings helps keep them real so you can address them. Acknowledging them doesn't strengthen them—it weakens them. Reflect on the connection between thoughts and feelings. How do yours relate to each other?

_____

_____

_____

_____

_____

Worries are negative thoughts about the future. Thinking of alternative possibilities can take the punch out of your worries. What things do you worry about most? Describe them, and then write alternative possibilities. You'll see that worried thoughts aren't guarantees.

_____

_____

_____

_____

_____

_____

_____

_____

_____

_____

_____

Talking about your anxiety (venting) can be very helpful. In the square on the left, list people you wouldn't mind reaching out to, then circle one or two of the names to start with. In the square on the right, jot down where you'll meet, what you'll do, and when you will connect with them.

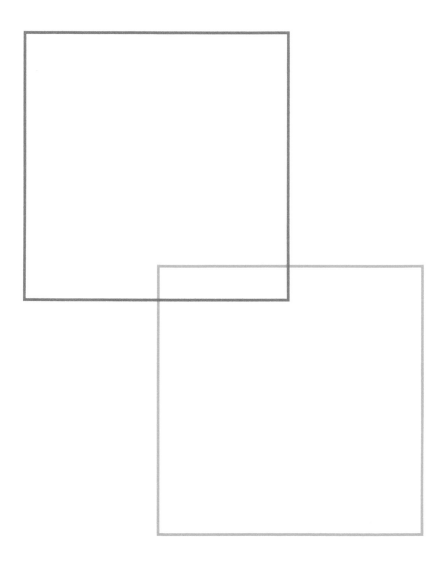

Do you have difficulty sleeping because of all your negative thoughts and anxieties? Reclaim your z's by changing your midnight thoughts. What can you think about instead of what's keeping you awake? Write down as many alternative thoughts as you can so when your brain gets negative in the night, you have something different to think about instead.

_____

_____

_____

_____

_____

_____

"You don't have to control your thoughts. You just have to stop letting them control you."

—DAN MILLMAN

Why do you want to change your thinking patterns? What motivates you to make the change?

_____

_____

_____

_____

_____

For you, what's the difference between acknowledging and understanding your thoughts and controlling them? How comfortable are you with the idea that we can't control our thoughts?

_____

_____

_____

_____

_____

You have a strong mind-body connection. What happens to one, manifests in the other. When your body is stiff and sore, what is often going on in your mind? How do your beliefs affect you physically? Reflect on your mind-body connection here.

_____

_____

_____

_____

_____

_____

_____

_____

_____

_____

What is your negativity bias like? Reflect on the recurring themes and subjects of your thoughts. Once you are aware of your particular biases, you can reframe them. Consider them from a new perspective, and rewrite them to be more positive and realistic.

_____

_____

_____

_____

_____

_____

_____

_____

_____

_____

Close your eyes and think of a negative, anxious thought. Sit with it. Scan your body from your toes to the top of your head, noting what you feel in each area. Draw how you feel (in a way that's meaningful to you) on the left side of the page. Next, close your eyes and breathe deeply. Think of something positive and empowering. Do the same scan. How do you feel this time? Draw the feeling on the right side of the page.

When you think about yourself, what types of thoughts do you have? Do the thoughts follow some of the ANT patterns? Which ones? What effect does your self-talk have on your anxiety?

_____

_____

_____

_____

_____

Describe yourself without such a strong negativity bias. You don't have to pretend you're perfect (because no one is), but challenge those negative beliefs about who you are and replace them with realistic descriptions.

_____

_____

_____

_____

_____

ANTs create negative, anxious beliefs about ourselves, our lives, and the world. To change this skewed perspective, look around you. Describe something that makes you smile or fills you with warmth. Then, write down a couple of statements of gratitude for that thing. Appreciating what's right overpowers what's wrong.

_____

_____

_____

_____

_____

_____

_____

_____

_____

_____

_____

T.H.I.N.K. before you believe, respond, feel, or act. This acronym is a self-check tool to test your thoughts. In response to anxiety, identify a thought. Consider if it's *true, helpful, inspirational, necessary,* and *kind.* If the answer to any of these categories is no, replace that thought with something more positive and realistic. Try it now. Write down a thought, and T.H.I.N.K. it through. Rewrite it if necessary.

_____

_____

_____

_____

_____

_____

_____

_____

_____

_____

"Ah, that's where I left my crippling fear of revolving doors!"

chapter three
MEAN-GIRL YOUR THOUGHTS

Have you seen the movie *Mean Girls*? It's quite a statement about relational aggression and, surprisingly, a source of inspiration for anyone being bullied by their anxious thoughts. The story involves a burn book, a journal filled with insults, lies, and other horrors. Sound familiar? I think it sounds just like our very own anxious thoughts. Like the characters in *Mean Girls*, you can steal and reveal anxiety's burn book containing your negative thoughts.

In this chapter, you'll expose your negative thoughts. The prompts will help you "mean-girl" those thoughts by laughing, mocking, refuting, and replacing the lies with accurate thoughts about yourself.

Have Your People Call My People: Your Thoughts Meet Reality

Everyone has core beliefs that shape their thoughts about themselves and their world. Alarmingly, about 70 to 80 percent of these beliefs are negative, such as "I'm no good" or "People only look out for themselves."

Core beliefs are based on how we interpreted things as kids, so they're neither factual nor objective. Children look to parents, other adults, and peers to learn about themselves and their world. A child whose parents ignore him and don't spend quality time with him learns that he isn't worthy of love and positive attention. Undoubtedly, as he grows, he'll have positive and negative experiences that shape his self-concept, but because the negative message about his worth formed early, was repeated often, and came from his parents, his core belief impacts his relationships with others and himself. For him, and for all of us, our core beliefs from childhood aren't even relevant anymore! These inaccurate viewpoints are in cahoots with the automatic negative thoughts we explored in chapter 2. Core beliefs and ANTs distort the way you see yourself and affect how you act in your world.

It's time to hang up on those beliefs. You're about to change your connections by questioning your thoughts and finding better, realistic answers. Hello, beliefs and thoughts? It's reality calling.

Stand Up to Your Thoughts or They'll Walk All over You

As we've learned, our thoughts can't be trusted. You've begun to question them, but that's only part of the gradual—and steady—process of regaining control over your own thoughts. Because you no longer fully believe your thoughts, you're ready for more action. You're ready to stand strong against anxiety.

Try this visualization exercise to practice standing fast against anxious thoughts.

1. Stand up tall.

2. Visualize yourself holding a stop sign.

3. On the stop sign you've written one limit you're placing on your thoughts right now.

4. What is that limit? What are you standing up to first?

A Stopped Clock Is Right Twice a Day

It's true that our thoughts can't be trusted. For this reason, it's important to get them out into the open, question them, and reshape them.

Sometimes, though, our ANTs are accurate. For instance, if you're competing with a coworker for a promotion and your anxious thoughts rev up, telling you that you'll "never be promoted," that could be a nudge telling you to determine what you want and what you need to do to get it.

To disagree with every anxious thought isn't helpful, and it just might keep you stuck. To move toward what you value requires a healthy perspective on the accuracy of your thoughts. Then, you can reject them or face them; either way, you're doing something about them.

Use Your Brain to Change Your Brain

The brain can seem like a mysterious entity that runs itself and takes us along for the ride. However, your brain is *you*. You're not disconnected from your operating system. Not only that, you are the programmer. You can make it think what you want it to think.

On its own, your brain can run amok, getting you into sticky situations that attract a colony of ANTs. You can regain control of your brain and your thoughts. Changing deeply ingrained negative thought patterns is a gradual but steady process of increasing awareness of your thoughts, challenging them, and determining positive, realistic thoughts and actions.

It's time to shape the thoughts you want to pay attention to.

> "As a conscious adult, you can choose to believe differently about yourself and about the world."
>
> —DOUGLAS BLOCH

What kind of person do you think you are? Ponder this, and for the next few minutes write down your answers.

_____

_____

_____

_____

_____

Look back at what you just wrote. What themes or patterns stand out to you? (Some common themes people have about themselves are "I'm worthless," "I'm unlovable," or "I'm annoying." There are many other themes, of course.)

_____

_____

_____

_____

_____

You may recall these themes (core beliefs) from way back in your childhood. They become our script for ourselves, one that we rehearse in our minds ad nauseam and act out in our lives. If you could rewrite the script (you can, and you will!), what would be different?

_____

_____

_____

_____

_____

_____

_____

_____

_____

_____

Remember the mean girls and their burn book? What's in your burn book? Look at the core beliefs and themes you wrote about earlier. How are these negative thoughts "burning" (harming) you? Jot down your thoughts about this, and then draw yourself burning your book of insults and enjoying the freedom it brings.

_____

_____

_____

_____

_____

Describe a time when one of your automatic negative thoughts was true. How did you deal with it?

_____

_____

_____

_____

_____

_____

_____

_____

_____

_____

_____

_____

Write down one of your negative thoughts or core beliefs about yourself. On a scale from 1 to 10, with 10 being the most accurate, how accurate do you think your negative thought or core belief is? Why did you choose this number?

1   2   3   4   5   6   7   8   9   10

_____

_____

_____

_____

_____

_____

> ## "Learning too soon our limitations, we never learn our powers."
>
> **—MIGNON MCLAUGHLIN**

If someone told you that you had powers, how would you respond? And what if someone else said you didn't have powers, just problems? How would you respond to that?

_____

_____

_____

_____

_____

_____

_____

_____

_____

_____

_____

You don't have to believe everything you think! Write down one negative thought you have about yourself or someone/something in your life. Now, list as many reasons as you can to prove that you don't have to believe this thought.

_____

_____

_____

_____

_____

_____

_____

_____

_____

_____

_____

If you could make one change to your anxious thoughts and their influence on you and your life, what would it be? How firmly do you believe that you can make the change happen? Whether you believe in yourself a little or a lot, the next step is the same: What is one small thing you will do today to work toward that change?

_____

_____

_____

_____

_____

_____

_____

_____

_____

_____

You discover on social media that someone you considered a friend (we'll call her Kyle) threw a party and didn't invite you. What's the first thing that pops into your mind?

a. Why am I never included? Why does everyone hate me? I don't want to keep seeing them all be so happy without me, so I'm deleting my social media accounts.

b. Oh my gosh! That time I was in the grocery store and I saw Kyle down the aisle but was in a hurry, so I pretended I didn't see her? That's what I did wrong! No wonder she didn't invite me. If I were Kyle, I'd be angry. I need to send her a fruit basket and a note of apology.

c. Good for Kyle for having a party! I know how stressed she's been, so she really deserved some relaxing fun with friends. This was about Kyle and what she needed. It wasn't about me. If she didn't want me there, I'm so happy that she didn't feel obligated to invite me.

One of those reactions was probably closer to your actual response than the others, but it wasn't fully yours. Describe what your true reaction would be: What would your thoughts be? How would you feel? What would you do about how you felt?

_____

_____

_____

_____

_____

_____

_____

_____

_____

_____

_____

A reason we all hold on to our negative core beliefs or our ANTs is because they are somewhat helpful to us despite the misery they cause. Write down one of the negative beliefs you have about yourself or others. What is an advantage to hanging on to it? What are the advantages of changing it?

_____

_____

_____

_____

_____

_____

"Stop letting people
who do so little for you
control so much of your mind,
feelings and emotions."

—WILL SMITH

You're outside when a neighbor drives by without waving. What goes through your mind? Describe how you might feel in this situation, physically and emotionally.

_____

_____

_____

_____

_____

_____

_____

_____

_____

_____

Are you absolutely sure that your thoughts about the waving incident are accurate? Maybe there are other explanations, things that have more to do with your neighbor than with you. List as many alternative possibilities as you can, even outlandish ones such as "That wasn't my neighbor. It was an alien in disguise." Then, circle anything that really could be possible.

_____

_____

_____

_____

_____

_____

_____

_____

_____

_____

_____

It can feel like we're always stressed and anxious, but anxiety waxes and wanes. Reflect on your anxious thoughts and feelings. When are they better? What is different during those times?

_____

_____

_____

_____

_____

_____

_____

_____

_____

_____

_____

_____

_____

Just because you think something, that doesn't make it real. In the space below, draw the most hideous monster you can imagine.

Your mind envisioned this monster, and your hand trans-ferred it to the page—it acted on a thought. Your mind will think of all sorts of monsters, but like this monster, they're not real. You don't have to pick up a pen to make them real.

What might happen when you stand up to your thoughts without backing down?

_____

_____

_____

_____

_____

_____

_____

_____

_____

_____

_____

Try an experiment. Go somewhere where there are people (e.g., your place of work, a grocery store, or a park). Choose someone. Write down what they're thinking. Repeat this a few more times. How do you know if you're right or wrong? Instead of trying to read minds, what would be a better use of your energy?

_____

_____

_____

_____

_____

_____

"Some people grumble that roses have thorns; I am grateful that thorns have roses."

—JEAN-BAPTISTE ALPHONSE KARR

Time for a self-check. What are you thinking about right now? List everything, even if it's vague. Describe your anxiety in this moment.

_____

_____

_____

_____

_____

Our negative thoughts can be brutal, and make us hard on ourselves. On the left, list words or phrases your ANTs use to describe you. On the right, stomp on those ANTs and change the words. Use positive, reality-based words to describe yourself.

_____   _____

_____   _____

_____   _____

_____   _____

_____   _____

On a scale from 1 to 10, with 10 representing extreme interference, how much is anxious thinking interfering with the quality of your life? What would it take to move the level of interference down the scale one point?

1	2	3	4	5	6	7	8	9	10

_____

_____

_____

_____

_____

_____

_____

_____

_____

_____

You are not a passive bystander! Part of standing up to your thoughts is doing things, step-by-step, to reduce the power your thoughts have over you. This can involve distancing yourself, shifting your attention, doing something active, or anything else that zaps stress and anxiety. Place a check mark beside the strategies you will try as a way to stand up to your thoughts. Add ideas of your own, too.

☐ Repeat, "I'm just having the thought that _____. That doesn't make it true."

☐ Visualize your thoughts crammed into a clown car and driving away.

☐ Take a brisk walk and shift your focus from your thoughts to the real world around you.

☐ Write a kind note (on paper, not a text) to someone positive in your life, describing positive things about them.

☐ Write a kind note (also on paper) to yourself, describing positive things about yourself. Use it to replace some of your ANTs.

☐ Do something fun, and immerse yourself in it. Return your attention to the activity when you notice your thoughts interrupting.

☐ _____

☐ _____

☐ _____

When you have thoughts consumed with worry and continue to think about them, they grow and take up more of your time, energy, and attention. Shifting your focus to different, positive, realistic thoughts helps change your thought patterns. What are some things you will shift your attention to when you catch yourself with ANTs?

_____

_____

_____

_____

_____

_____

_____

_____

_____

_____

Anxious thoughts are like caffeinated hamsters on a wheel. Hop off the wheel! It's necessary to have something to jump to, or there's nothing to replace your spinning thoughts with. What will be waiting for you to take the place of negative thoughts?

_____

_____

_____

_____

_____

We can't choose all of our thoughts, but we can choose how we react to them. When faced with anxious thoughts, how do you usually react? What is the result? What could you choose to do instead?

_____

_____

_____

_____

_____

Too often, our core beliefs about ourselves are negative and downright mean. Affirmations, positive statements about who we are, change our brain and our thoughts. An affirmation is a single sentence starting with "I am." Write affirmations on separate slips of paper and place them where you'll see them through your day. Start now by writing at least five positive affirmations. These examples will help you begin.

I am qualified to do my job.
I am a good parent because I take time for my kids.

1. _____

_____

2. _____

_____

3. _____

_____

4. _____

_____

5. _____

_____

"Once I'm mindful enough, I'll get some pajamas my mom didn't pick out."

chapter four

"MINDFULNESS." OPRAH KEEPS SAYING THAT WORD

Mindfulness seems to be the flashy, trendy wellness word of choice. Even Oprah touts its effectiveness for all things well-being. Oprah is correct, but mindfulness isn't a passing trend. Mindfulness is an integral part of mental health and well-being, especially when it becomes a way of life rather than merely a tool to use. In a nutshell, mindfulness is paying attention to the present moment, your *now*.

While I do many things to keep my own anxiety where it belongs (as far away from me as possible), my favorite method is mindfulness. With it, I gently return my thoughts to my now, and away from worries about the past and future—even if my worries are about something that happened a minute ago or might happen a minute from now. About the only things you need for practicing mindfulness are patience and a willingness to pay attention to the present moment.

Mindfulness is something you cultivate from within you. It is a practice—a state of existence, really—that you willfully engage in to replace stress and anxiety with serenity and calm. In this chapter, we'll embark on a mindful journey to learn mindfulness meditations and habits to help with anxiety.

Mindfulness: Not Just for People Doing Yoga in Pharmaceutical Commercials

Mindfulness does not mean the absence of anxious thoughts, stress, and problems. It's a way of creating contentment and fulfillment in your life despite the negative. Mindfulness is a way of being, a way of experiencing yourself and your world. To be mindful is to pay attention completely. When you live mindfully, you show up for yourself and your life—right here, right now.

One of the many beautiful things about mindfulness is that it's for everyone, including you. Practicing mindfulness doesn't require anything other than a decision by you to connect with your now in order to live freely and well, unhindered by stress and anxiety.

You'll soon learn about and engage in lots of different mindfulness exercises. The possibilities for cultivating a mindful way of life are abundant, so you can replace stress and anxiety with mindfulness activities that you like.

Scan Your Body for More Than Just Irregular Moles

Wrestling with anxiety is frustrating. Does this cycle look familiar?

You experience anxiety and stress → You want them out of your life → Your focus remains on what you *don't want* → You think about them often ↑

You can break this cycle! Anxiety and stress hang on (and on and on) because that's what we're thinking about. Even if we're thinking about overcoming them, they're on our minds. To break the cycle, you have to shift your attention.

Shifting is possible with mindfulness and meditation, scanning and noticing. To somewhat oversimplify, mindfulness involves attending to what your senses notice about the world around you, while meditation involves noticing and releasing your inner experience.

You're about to break your vicious cycle with some meditations and mindfulness practices. Get ready to scan, notice, and shift!

Tune In to Your Body: It's Lonely

We're born whole: The mind and body are one. When you were an infant, you knew how to listen to your body and communicate your needs. You were mindful by nature, living only in the present moment.

As adults, many of us have lost that intimate communion of body and mind. We might have anxious thoughts, and we might have physical symptoms anywhere in the body. However, too often we keep thoughts and sensations in separate jars to be addressed independently.

Mindfulness and meditation reunite mind and body and offer tremendous potential for stress and anxiety relief. The following exercises will help you be present with mind and body to swap problems with peace.

"Meditation does not involve trying to change your thinking by thinking some more. It involves watching thought itself."

—JON KABAT-ZINN, *WHEREVER YOU GO, THERE YOU ARE: MINDFULNESS MEDITATION IN EVERYDAY LIFE*

Begin to watch and observe. Take this journal outside or to a favorite room indoors. For several minutes, slowly scan your area. What is in your surroundings? Take it all in. Now jot down what your eyes notice, but don't judge or describe. Simply see and scrawl.

_____

_____

_____

_____

_____

_____

_____

_____

_____

_____

_____

You can be mindful of the tiniest of things. It's all about intention: What do you want to pay attention to right now? Give it a try. Find something small—maybe a coin, button, or pebble—and hold it in your hand. Observe it for a few minutes, this time adding your sense of touch to your sight. Now, scribble down the details about what you saw and felt.

_____

_____

_____

_____

_____

_____

_____

_____

_____

_____

Thought Balloons

* Choose a location, remove all distractions—including your phone—and settle into a comfortable seat.

* Close your eyes and begin to breathe slowly and deeply.

* Place one hand on your rib cage and the other on your belly to feel the rise and fall of your breath.

* You are likely having thoughts, perhaps many different ones. That's normal. Rather than resisting, watch them without latching on to them.

* Visualize your thoughts becoming colorful balloons. They're no longer part of you.

* Smile as you watch these thought balloons float up, up, and away.

* Allow any lingering balloons to drift as you return your attention to your breath.

* Slowly open your eyes.

Describe what it was like for you to simply observe your thoughts, watching them float away without being carried away with them. What will life be like for you as you become adept at doing this?

_____

_____

_____

_____

_____

_____

_____

_____

_____

_____

_____

_____

Your Anxiety-Free Zone

* As before, remove distractions and settle into a comfortable seat.

* Close your eyes and begin to breathe slowly, deeply.

* Feel your body move with your breath.

* Visualize a place, real or imaginary, where you're free from anxiety and stress.

* Picture yourself in this place. What does it look like? Design it in your mind's eye.

* What colors do you notice? Decorations? Objects?

* What scents do you smell?

* What sounds stand out?

* Be present here, enjoying freedom from anxiety.

* Return your attention to your breath. When ready, open your eyes.

Let's say you landed an interview for your dream job. Describe your thoughts and emotions about the upcoming interview. What specifically makes you anxious? How will you use mindfulness to be present and focused on the interview rather than on worries and fears?

_____

_____

_____

_____

_____

_____

_____

_____

_____

_____

"Knowing what you are doing while you are doing it is the essence of mindfulness practice."

—JON KABAT-ZINN,
FULL CATASTROPHE LIVING:
HOW TO COPE WITH STRESS,
PAIN AND ILLNESS USING
MINDFULNESS MEDITATION

When you're mindfully immersed in the moment, you can experience flow. The epitome of mindfulness, flow is being so thoroughly absorbed in an activity that all else, including problems, drop away from conscious thought. Knowing what activities make you feel happy and positive helps you achieve this. List activities you find fun and relaxing. Then circle one activity you will start doing now to experience mindful flow and happiness.

_____

_____

_____

_____

_____

_____

_____

_____

Mindfulness helps even when the present moment is stressful. Instead of focusing on the stressful circumstance, use mindfulness to tend to one neutral thing. Visualize something that reduces your stress, and study it in your imagination. Compile a list of things or people you can imagine when your present moment is rough.

_____

_____

_____

_____

_____

_____

_____

_____

_____

_____

Muscle Mindfulness

* Again, remove all distractions and settle into a comfortable seat.

* Close your eyes and begin to breathe slowly, deeply.

* With your hands resting lightly on your belly, tune in to its rise and fall.

* Tune in to your body. Where do you notice tension?

* Imagine your breath flowing into the tension, bringing warm, healing energy with your inhale and escorting toxic stress out with your exhale.

* Add touch to the experience by gently massaging the tense area.

* Visualize your inflamed muscle returning to its calm, smooth state, and feel the shift.

* Open your eyes, adjust your position, and smile.

* Commit to loving and caring for this spot.

Mindfulness shifts thoughts and changes emotional reactions.
It also leads to action, to effective new behaviors. When you face
problems, your actions often reflect your discontent and stress.
To make changes, be mindful of your actions. Describe a problem
you're having and how it's affecting you. Now, list three or four
effective new actions you could take to move toward improvement.

_____

_____

_____

_____

_____

_____

_____

_____

_____

_____

Worries and what-ifs can become the center of your thoughts and crowd out positive beliefs and ideas. If you're worried about a relationship ending, for example, shift your thoughts toward positive ideas and actions. Describe a worry, then list reasons not to worry. How will you use present-moment awareness to distance yourself from worries?

_____

_____

_____

_____

_____

_____

_____

_____

_____

_____

"Why do anxiety, stress, or negativity arise? Because you turned away from the present moment. And why did you do that? You thought something else was more important. One small error, one misperception, creates a world of suffering."

—ECKHART TOLLE,
*ONENESS WITH ALL LIFE:
INSPIRATIONAL SELECTIONS
FROM A NEW EARTH*

Reducing anxiety requires you to shift your focus away from what's wrong. This is possible when you know what is right for you. What do you want instead of anxiety? What is important to you?

_____

_____

_____

_____

Think of someone important to you. The very next time you're with him or her, what will you do to be fully present during your time together?

_____

_____

_____

_____

_____

_____

Affirm Who You Are

- Remove all distractions and settle into a comfortable seat.

- Close your eyes and begin to breathe slowly, deeply.

- Rest your fingertips an inch above your navel. Breathe deeply so your hands move out with each inhale and in with each exhale.

- Repeat one of these affirmations as you breathe:

  - I am more than my anxiety.
  - I am in control of my thoughts and emotions.
  - I choose positive, healthy actions.
  - I thrive even with anxiety in my life.
  - I am creating and enjoying a new way of being.
  - I show up fully for my life with present-moment awareness.

- Open your eyes and center yourself in the moment.

Boldly announcing to yourself who you are, what strengths you possess, and what you value encourages you to be mindful of these qualities every day. Begin your process of self-affirmation by thoughtfully completing each column.

I'M A PERSON WHO . . .	THESE ARE SOME OF MY CHARACTER STRENGTHS	THIS IS WHO AND WHAT IS IMPORTANT TO ME

Research has shown that affirmations aren't malarkey. They open you up to new possibilities and help you firmly believe in yourself. Use them in meditation, as you did previously, or write them down and carry them with you. Start a compilation of affirmations that resonate with you. Use the ones from page 106, or write your own.

Helpful hint: Affirmations are most effective when they are action-oriented and written in the present tense. "I thrive even with anxiety in my life" is stronger than "I don't let anxiety stop me."

_____

_____

_____

_____

_____

_____

_____

_____

_____

Taste is a sense that is often overlooked in mindfulness, for obvious reasons (when hiking, for example, tasting things as you go is not a good idea). It's still a valuable practice, though. Use taste to ground you in the moment with something as simple and portable as gum. Practice experiencing taste mindfully by chewing gum or substituting something edible on hand. Write down what you experience.

"Stress is an ignorant state.
It believes everything is
an emergency."

—NATALIE GOLDBERG

Anxiety and stress can send you into a state of alertness. Mindfulness does the opposite, inducing and maintaining calm. Grow still when you're freaking out, identify things that soothe, and attend to them mindfully, one by one. Practice now. Look around, let your eyes fall on objects, use your senses, and list and describe what you find calming.

_____

_____

_____

_____

_____

_____

_____

_____

_____

_____

Non-judgment is an important aspect of mindfulness. Anxiety judges everything, filling our minds with evaluations that cause fear and more anxiety. Mindfulness teaches and fosters openness. You begin to simply be, seeing, hearing, feeling, smelling, and even tasting with present-moment awareness. As you begin to exist without judging, your anxiety will shrink.

Melt Away Your Thoughts

* As before, remove all distractions and settle into a comfortable seat.

* Close your eyes and begin to breathe slowly, deeply.

* Listen to the air as it enters your nose.

* Visualize yourself outside on a summer day.

* Imagine your anxious thoughts as ice cubes in a pitcher of tea in front of you.

* Watch them slowly melt away.

* Eyes still closed, mindfully take in your surroundings. What do you see? Hear? Smell? Feel?

* Picture these images as fresh, new ice cubes.

* Pour yourself a glass and enjoy it mindfully.

* Open your eyes and smile.

Anxiety hooks us like a fish snagged by a fisherman's lure. Unhook yourself with mindfulness. Instead of thrashing about, breathe and turn your attention elsewhere. Write about something that has hooked you. What can you attend to instead? How will you know when you've slipped off the hook?

_____

_____

_____

_____

_____

_____

_____

_____

_____

_____

Living mindfully and intentionally, with purpose and meaning, is one of the most powerful ways to have anxiety and thrive anyway. Reflect on what you hold dear. What are you passionate about? What does living with purpose look like for you?

Cultivate a Beginner's Mind

* As before, remove all distractions and settle into a comfortable seat.

* Close your eyes and begin to breathe slowly, deeply.

* Touch your shoulders and notice if they rise and fall when you breathe. If so, breathe more deeply so that your belly rises and falls instead.

* Picture a young child.

* This child is with her parents, about to enter a toy store for the first time.

* You are now in the store, observing this child.

* Note her expression, her exclamations, her actions.

* Imagine something that brings you such delight.

* Suddenly, you can capture that delight, that first-time-in-a-toy-store feeling.

* Visualize yourself living with delight in any situation.

* Open your eyes and smile.

A beginner has no expectations or past experiences to color a moment. There's no reason for anxiety, fear, or stress. "Beginner's mind" refers to the state of being fresh, new to an experience. Name an anxiety-provoking situation. Imagine it with a beginner's mind. With no preconceived notions, what do you take in with your senses? How would beginner's mind change your experience?

_____

_____

_____

_____

_____

_____

_____

_____

_____

_____

Mindfulness is even effective in heavy traffic when you're in a hurry. It involves using your senses to pull you away from anxiety and be calm in a stressful moment. Observing your surroundings will divert your attention from anxious thoughts. How can you use mindfulness to stay relaxed when you're in the car?

"No matter where you are on your journey, that's exactly where you need to be."

—OPRAH WINFREY

"I came here for coffee and stayed for the terrifying small talk.
I don't even know what a flat white is!"

chapter five
LEAVE YOUR HOUSE

One of anxiety's biggest tragedies is the limitations it places on people and the way they live their lives. Anxiety uses fear, worries, and what-ifs to control you, keeping you away from people, places, and situations. Anxiety robs people of joy and even keeps them trapped in their homes.

I'd like to give you a different perspective to consider. Avoidance is a choice. Realizing this puts you back in control. You're not at anxiety's mercy, and you can decide to participate fully in your life again.

In this chapter, you'll learn about gradual exposure, a proven technique for reducing anxiety and avoidance. You'll use exposure and exploration to have fun freeing yourself from anxiety's limits.

Go Outside and Do Scary Things

Fear itself isn't the problem: our reaction to fear and anxiety is. You can learn to choose different actions beyond avoidance. Regardless of your specific fears and worries, an effective and safe way to learn new responses is through gradual exposure.

Facing fear can be scary and intimidating at first, so if you're hesitant, that's okay! Exposure to fears and worries is a process that makes you become increasingly comfortable. Over time you will no longer need to avoid your fears and will be free to choose different behaviors in the face of anxiety. The more you do it, the easier it will get!

Gradual exposure does the following:

* Targets avoidance behavior

* Allows you to challenge anxiety in manageable chunks

* Gradually moves you forward to break away from your limitations

* Increases your control over what you do and the person you want to be

Just as you've been confronting your thoughts and feelings, you'll stand up to fear and avoidance by journaling your way through this chapter.

Face Your Anxiety from the Comfort of Your Own Home

Gradual exposure to your fears is effective, and there are other helpful techniques, too. Thought exercises like you've been doing in this book allow you to examine, grapple with, and question your anxious thoughts.

There are many ways to destroy anxiety. You can even think it away in your favorite chair at home. Thought exercises involve probing questions that help get anxiety out of your head and onto paper so you can challenge it. As you identify problems, you'll discover new things about yourself: your unique thoughts and beliefs about anxiety, how they're limiting you, and what you want to replace them with.

Your Worst Fear Realized: The Barista Remembered You

Many people living with anxiety don't want to stand out. If you are among the anxiety sufferers who want to remain inconspicuous, It might be horrifying to think that someone from a coffee shop would recognize you later. An aversion to being noticed and, possibly, judged can send someone right into avoidance mode.

Exposure therapy will diminish fears, but initially it might increase anxiety. That barista might come right up to you and start a conversation. You might attempt to talk to her, but you think you sound ridiculous. Your anxiety skyrockets, and you want to hide.

We often feel anxious about something important to us. Your worry about botching a conversation could be reminding you that you want to form friendships. When your values drive exposure, anxiety can't hold you back.

Ready? Let's dive in to some exposure scenarios and thought exercises!

> "People have a hard time letting go of their suffering. Out of a fear of the unknown, they prefer suffering that is familiar."
>
> —THICH NHAT HANH

Describe one fear or worry that is limiting your life. How is it restricting you?

_____

_____

_____

_____

_____

Who and/or what do you tend to avoid? What do you think you'll have to experience if you face the situation?

_____

_____

_____

_____

_____

Avoidance can begin as dodging a single situation or person that makes you anxious, and from there expand until it's a habit that dictates all the things you can't do. List the places, people, and activities you've been avoiding because of anxiety. Then, rank them from most to least anxiety provoking. Circle the one you will stop avoiding first, ideally one of your least bothersome situations.

_____

_____

_____

_____

_____

_____

_____

_____

_____

_____

Consider the item you just circled. How do you feel about using gradual exposure to lift the limits it has imposed on you?

a. It's cool. I only avoid it so I don't have to get dressed.

b. I feel keyed up, on edge. I don't like feeling this way, so I'm not sure about going through with exposure.

c. I feel ill. I'm pretty sure that if I try to stop avoiding it even a little, I will projectile vomit on people or suffocate or have a heart attack. I know I can't handle this fear, so I will just keep avoiding it.

d. Other. Write it here: _____

Reactions are automatic; they are instinctive actions based on emotions. Responses, in contrast, are more deliberate and based on rational choices. Do you find yourself reacting to your fears rather than responding to them? Name a fear or anxiety-provoking situation.

HOW HAVE YOU BEEN REACTING TO IT?	WHAT CHOICES DO YOU HAVE INSTEAD?

Avoidance is a reaction, and you've been doing it for good reason. Reacting to anxiety by avoiding it is natural and doesn't mean you're weak or "bad." It is, however, an unhealthy reaction that negatively impacts your life. Describe how you feel physically and emotionally when you have the urge to react by avoidance.

_____

_____

_____

_____

_____

_____

"Life is 10 percent what happens to you and 90 percent how you respond to it."

—LOU HOLTZ

Are your physical and emotional symptoms of anxiety bad enough to keep you trapped in a life of fear and avoidance? Why or why not?

_____

_____

_____

_____

_____

_____

_____

_____

_____

_____

_____

_____

One of the dangerous effects of anxiety is that it can zap the joy right out of you. As you practice exposure to intimidating things, don't forget to add exposure to fun and positivity. When getting out or staying in, what do you like to do? What would you like to try? Who do you have fun with? Draw pictures of your ideas here.

Make this pledge to yourself: *Step-by-step, I will face what makes me anxious, worried, or afraid.* Now, write the pledge on paper (and decorate it!) to keep with you. On a scale from 1 to 10, with 10 being the most, how much do you believe in your ability to face your anxieties? What will it take for you to move up just one number on that scale? How will you do it?

1   2   3   4   5   6   7   8   9   10

_____

_____

_____

_____

_____

_____

_____

_____

_____

Tackling anxiety step-by-step involves doing one thing every day to chip away at it. There's no time like the present moment to start. What will you do today to respond to anxiety rather than react to it? When will you do it? When you've done it, return to your journal and describe what the experience was like.

_____

_____

_____

_____

_____

_____

"Whether you think you can, or you think you can't— you're right."

—HENRY FORD

How often do your fears come true? When they do, what's the worst thing that happens?

_____

_____

_____

_____

_____

Remember a recent encounter when you felt high anxiety. How did you get through it?

_____

_____

_____

_____

_____

_____

_____

In the left circle, write down five things you'll do more of when you shrink your anxiety. In the right circle, write five things you'll do less of.

Set a timer for one minute. Close your eyes and imagine a situation you want to avoid. Picture it in detail. What do you see? Hear? Smell? Feel? Who's there? What's happening? Override your desire to leave, and remain there until your timer chimes. Describe how you were able to stay as long as you did.

_____

_____

_____

_____

Repeat the exercise, this time setting your timer for three minutes. Call to mind the same situation you want to avoid. Capture the details. Remain there until your timer chimes. Describe how the three-minute exposure compared to the one-minute practice. Why might there have been differences?

_____

_____

_____

_____

"The biggest adventure
you can take is to live
the life of your dreams."

—OPRAH WINFREY

What is the life of your dreams? How will you develop the courage to embark on the adventure?

_____

_____

_____

You're in a pool, and you have a beach ball. On the beach ball are words representing negative thoughts and emotions. You don't like those thoughts and emotions, so you push the beach ball underwater. It keeps popping up, and you keep pushing it down. Tired, you let go, and it floats nearby. Draw yourself in a pool with floating beach balls. How will you stay in there when you're surrounded by all this anxiety? (Hint: There is a lot of water between the beach balls. What does that water represent to you?)

Letting go of the beach ball and avoiding situations are not the same. When you release the ball, you are free to swim even though the ball is still floating around. When you avoid, you bolt out of the pool and stand on the side shivering, dripping, and missing the fun. List at least five reasons to stay in a situation even though your symptoms won't go away.

1. _____

_____

2. _____

_____

3. _____

_____

4. _____

_____

5. _____

_____

Anxiety in the body can trigger avoidance; use exposure to the physical symptoms of anxiety to become more accustomed to them. In the left column, list some ways your body tells you you're anxious. In the right column, list exposure practices that will increase your tolerance of these symptoms. Use these examples for ideas.

MY SYMPTOM	EXPOSURE EXERCISE
Heart pounding in chest	*Run up and down steps or around the house, then sit with the feeling.*
Difficulty swallowing	*Eat raw broccoli or plain bread (with a glass of water nearby).*

If someone you care about were in your shoes, how would you help them with their avoidance? In what ways will you apply this help and compassion to yourself?

_____

_____

_____

_____

_____

Separating yourself from your anxiety helps lessen its control over you. Part of separation is boldly dismissing it and confidently saying goodbye and good riddance. Write a goodbye letter to your anxiety and all that it represents.

_____

_____

_____

_____

_____

With gradual exposure practice, you begin to believe in your ability to break free from anxiety and soar past its limits. To gain that freedom, track your activities and successes, even if you think they're small. (No success is ever small; each one is a step in the right direction.) Recording your victories is empowering, and having a daily chart keeps you accountable every day. Use one on page 140 for practice, and then make your own and keep going!

	SUNDAY	MONDAY	TUESDAY
Situation I Wanted to Avoid			
How I Used Exposure			
Why I Wanted to Stay			
How I Found the Strength to Stay Despite Anxiety			

WEDNESDAY	THURSDAY	FRIDAY	SATURDAY

	SUNDAY	MONDAY	TUESDAY
Responses to Anxiety and Actions I Took			
On a Scale from 1 to 10 (10 is the Most), How Proud of Myself Am I?			
On a Scale from 1 to 10, How Much Do I Think I Can Withstand Anxiety in This Situation Again?			
Other Remarks or Observations			

WEDNESDAY	THURSDAY	FRIDAY	SATURDAY

Anxiety is part of the human experience. Just as that beach ball was still in the pool, anxiety will stay in your pool. That's okay. Anxiety is an alert for what's important to us, and it propels us to act when necessary. When you no longer avoid it, you can forge a healthy relationship with it. How will your life be when you can swim in the same pool as your anxiety?

\
\
\
\
\
\
\
\
\

"*I always knew the key to inner peace was hydration.*"

chapter six

DO THE STUFF TV DOCTORS TELL YOU TO DO

Some of that stuff on TV isn't fiction, including those shows that have caring doctors helping their patients live well. I'm not a doctor, but I do care and want you to live your best life. Your anxiety relief journal wraps up by focusing on a healthy lifestyle for genuine well-being. All of the work you've done in your journal is more than a collection of exercises to be completed and then forgotten. Your self-worth is far more than that! Together, these chapters guide you to create a quality life.

In this chapter, you'll dive in to prompts and exercises for shaping a healthy way of life.

All That Self-Care Business

Sometimes, the thought of adopting a healthy lifestyle is both daunting and annoying. Can't we just do the other stuff—mindfulness, working on thoughts, exposure practice—and call it good enough? Possibly. But the question then becomes, "What does 'good enough' mean to you and your life?"

You have the power to choose your answer to that question and achieve optimum well-being. Creating your well-lived life, one of physical and mental health, involves caring deeply for yourself and your wellness. This self-care has many facets that work in concert so you can be the way you want to be.

Take a glimpse into some major realms of self-care in the folowing chart:

SELF-CARE ACTIVITY	HOW IT HELPS	EXAMPLES
Eating right	Nurtures the brain-gut axis (a direct channel of communication between the brain and gut). Nutrients increase biochemicals like serotonin (did you know that over 90 percent of our serotonin receptors are in the gut?) and decrease stress hormones like cortisol and adrenaline.	Celery, asparagus, lettuce, green beans, beets, onions, garlic, peaches, berries, citrus fruits, bananas, whole grains, nuts, seeds, egg yolks, salmon, oysters

SELF-CARE ACTIVITY	HOW IT HELPS	EXAMPLES
Drinking water	Essential for your brain, which is about 80 percent water. Water increases blood flow, balances mood, and chases away fatigue.	Plain, pure water is the best thing you can drink to boost your brain and keep anxiety at bay.
Sleep	About 7 to 8 hours of quality sleep removes toxins that accumulate when you're awake, keeps brain cells communicating with each other, and forges neural pathways. Anxiety and stress are minimized, and negative experiences are easier to process and handle.	Develop and use a sleep routine. Go to bed around the same time every night, and get up at the same time each morning. Turn off screens two hours before bed, and begin wind-down activities like yoga, mindfulness meditation, light reading, or aromatherapy.
Exercise	Just five short minutes of aerobic exercise can have anti-anxiety effects! Exercise releases endorphins (the feel-good hormone), improves sleep, and lowers stress and tension.	Any movement counts, especially when you're just beginning. The key is to do what you enjoy. Enjoyment is part of a quality life.

SELF-CARE ACTIVITY	HOW IT HELPS	EXAMPLES
Relaxation	Allowing your brain to rest and rejuvenate keeps it happy and less prone to anxiety. When brain and body relax together, well-being deepens.	Choose calming, pleasurable activities. Yoga is particularly relaxing. You can find a relaxing, low-key hobby, meditate, play with kinetic sand, or anything else that calms your mind and body.

Treating your whole self with respect and loving-kindness effectively reduces anxiety and provides a boost for your overall lifestyle of well-being.

That Fourth Cup of Coffee Probably Didn't Help

HALT! Do you need to stop some of the things you are doing in order to feel less anxious?

Think of HALTing certain anxiety-increasing activities. The acronym stands for hungry, angry, lonely, tired. When you notice yourself feeling especially anxious and stressed, run through the HALT feelings and address what you need to.

Beyond HALT, a diet of processed, fried, fatty, sugary foods and beverages, too much caffeine (some people have zero tolerance while others can handle one or two cups of coffee or black tea), and lack of exercise and other self-care activities are among anxiety's contributing factors.

The great thing about all of this, whether something is anxiety reducing or anxiety provoking, is that everything is in your control. You have the power to make choices that enhance your life. The following exercises will lead you down the healthy path you've already begun.

"Nothing diminishes anxiety faster than action."

—WALTER ANDERSON

Actions really do speak louder than words. Try this: Drop your pen. Think about picking it up. Where is the pen? Now take action and pick it up. With that pen in hand, jot down something you've been thinking about doing. What will it be like to do it rather than thinking or talking about doing it?

_____

_____

_____

_____

_____

_____

_____

_____

_____

_____

Describe what has been preventing you from moving forward. The thought of change, even positive change, causes discomfort. On a scale from 1 to 10, with 10 being the most, how much do you want to let go and move on?

_____

_____

_____

_____

_____

_____

_____

_____

_____

| 1 | 2 | 3 | 4 | 5 | 6 | 7 | 8 | 9 | 10 |

You are in control of your behaviors. You don't have to wait for anxiety to be gone before you live fully. What do you choose to start doing today? How will you do it despite the anxiety that's been holding you back?

_____

_____

_____

_____

_____

_____

_____

_____

_____

_____

Anxiety can make life feel daunting. Breaking things down into small, manageable steps helps you start accomplishing tasks. This applies for everything from a household chore to a professional goal, and then to a fun activity. Choose something that is overwhelming and anxiety provoking right now, and write it down as a goal. Thinking about the task in small pieces, list steps you need to take to do it.

GOAL

_____

_____

_____

_____

_____

_____

Many of us are enthusiastic about making changes and taking back our lives. The problem is the "P" word: procrastination. Write a slogan that describes your procrastination, such as "Don't do today what you can put off until tomorrow" or "I'll do it! Right after . . . " (That's one of mine.)

_____

_____

_____

Reflect on your procrastination motto. How has it been serving you? (There must be an advantage, or you wouldn't procrastinate.) How would changing the motto work better? Create a new motto. Write it here and also on a sheet of paper that you can put in a prominent place.

_____

_____

_____

_____

_____

We often eat on autopilot, grabbing what's convenient and tasty without fully paying attention to physical and mental health. Think about it and quickly scribble a list of what you've been eating and drinking recently.

_____

_____

_____

_____

_____

_____

> "The way you think, the way you behave, the way you eat, can influence your life by 30 to 50 years."
>
> —DEEPAK CHOPRA

Study your food and beverage list. Describe how you feel overall (mood, quality of thoughts, physical experiences). Diet plays a role in health and well-being. What could you eat/drink less of? More of?

_____

_____

_____

_____

_____

_____

_____

_____

_____

_____

_____

Your brain and body become slightly dehydrated overnight, causing you to wake up feeling anxious, groggy, tired, and generally unwell. For a better start to your day, drink at least eight ounces of water right away. Make it a priority to drink a glass or two of water in the morning. Describe the impact.

Write about a time when your anxiety was better. What was different then? How can you do more of what worked before?

A lack of routine can contribute to anxiety. Describe how your anxiety ebbs and flows during a typical day. Circle times (if they exist) when you aren't following a predictable routine. How can you create routines to decrease chaos?

_____

_____

_____

_____

_____

_____

_____

_____

_____

_____

Having a life philosophy to motivate and guide you is powerful and effective at helping you move forward despite anxiety. Start developing your own life philosophy. This process may seem difficult, but one has to start somewhere—and what better place than your anxiety journal? What is your outlook on your life?

_____

_____

_____

_____

_____

_____

_____

_____

_____

_____

_____

You probably don't want to spend your life dreading one day at a time. What would it take for you to look forward to one day at a time?

_____

_____

_____

_____

_____

_____

_____

_____

Eagerly anticipating the next day is wonderful. It does, however, take you out of *this* moment. Look around you and within you. List at least six reasons to be content right now.

Do this exercise often to keep you mindfully, happily anchored in the present.

1. _____

2. _____

3. _____

4. _____

5. _____

6. _____

Vision boards inspire and motivate, keeping your goals and dreams in sight. Create a mini vision board here. Choose a goal for your life or a concept of how you want to be. Sketch pictures that represent your vision, and include words or phrases that stand for what you want.

Self-care can involve activities that make us feel happy and relaxed, or it can include things that make us uncomfortable or anxious. This is good! Growth and change are challenging because they involve questioning long-held beliefs and replacing them with different ideas that we must get used to. In the left column, list self-care activities that you'll do to feel good. In the right column, list self-care activities for growth that make you uncomfortable.

COMFORTABLE	UNCOMFORTABLE

Growth includes changing habits. To change, replace your habit with something better. Jot down a few habits that you'd like to break to improve your life. Now, brainstorm as many replacements as you can. For example: *I push Snooze on my alarm too many times. I'll get up with the first alarm and have the time to mindfully enjoy a cup of tea.*

_____

_____

_____

_____

_____

_____

_____

_____

_____

_____

Reflect on mindfulness expert Jon Kabat-Zinn's words. What meaning do they have for you? Does his statement make you feel anxious or empowered?

_____

_____

_____

_____

_____

_____

_____

"Wherever you go,
there you are."

—JON KABAT-ZINN

The VIA Institute on Character has, through research, identified 24 character strengths that we all have to varying degrees. Read through this list and circle the 10 strengths that apply to you the most.

appreciation of beauty	hope	perseverance
bravery	humility	perspective
creativity	humor	prudence
curiosity	judgment	self-regulation
fairness	kindness	social intelligence
forgiveness	leadership	spirituality
gratitude	love	teamwork
honesty	love of learning	zest

Not using our character strengths can contribute to anxiety because we're not living in alignment with what we believe is important. Consider the strengths you circled. Are there some that you feel you're not using? What could you do differently to let your character strengths, not your anxiety, drive you?

_____

_____

_____

_____

_____

_____

_____

_____

_____

_____

The process of creating your quality life beyond anxiety isn't linear. You'll likely run into barriers in any direction you travel. Knowing what you're up against can help you prepare for road-blocks and know how to respond to them. Draw the obstacles you might encounter on your journey. Describe things you could do to get around the blockades.

_____

_____

_____

_____

_____

_____

Gratitude is a perspective, one of appreciation and thankfulness for the good in life. Seeing the good weakens negative thoughts and reduces anxiety because we focus on the positive in our lives. List as many things as you can, big and small, that you are glad about. Use this list to begin a dedicated gratitude journal.

_____

_____

_____

_____

_____

_____

_____

_____

_____

_____

_____

Rituals—meaningful activities done routinely and in the same fashion—can energize or calm, both feelings that inspire you to keep working to move past anxiety. One of my rituals is to sip tea mindfully—outside, if the weather permits. Create your own ritual. How do you want that ritual to make you feel? What will you do, and when will you do it? Brainstorm ideas here.

_____

_____

_____

_____

_____

_____

_____

_____

_____

_____

Your journal is now full of anxiety-reducing, life-living ideas that you've developed. Rather than trying them all at once, which would probably exacerbate anxiety and ANTs, dive in right away with one approach. Gradually add others at your own pace. Thumb through your journal. Choose one starting point. Write it here, and describe what, exactly, you'll do to create your quality life.

_____

_____

_____

_____

_____

_____

_____

_____

_____

_____

What will your life be like when you beat the limitations anxiety, fear, worry, and avoidance have placed on you? Think about relationships, work, fun and enjoyment, self-care, and self-love.

_____

_____

_____

_____

_____

_____

_____

_____

_____

_____

"Every breath we take, every step we take, can be filled with peace, joy, and serenity. The question is whether or not we are in touch with it. We need only to be awake, alive in the present moment."

—THICH NHAT HANH,
*PEACE IS EVERY STEP:
THE PATH OF MINDFULNESS
IN EVERYDAY LIFE*

RESOURCES

The following user-friendly resources offer additional information about anxiety and how you can stop freaking out and start living your life freely and fully.

Books

Be Calm: Proven Techniques to Stop Anxiety Now by Jill P. Weber, PhD (Althea Press, 2019)

Break Free: Acceptance and Commitment Therapy in 3 Steps: A Workbook for Overcoming Self-Doubt and Embracing Life by Tanya J. Peterson, MS, NCC (Althea Press, 2016)

Breathwork: A 3-Week Breathing Program to Gain Clarity, Calm, and Better Health by Valerie Moselle (Althea Press, 2019)

The Happiness Trap: How to Stop Struggling and Start Living: A Guide to ACT by Russ Harris (Trumpeter, 2008)

How to Live: Boxed Set of the Mindfulness Essentials Series by Thich Nhat Hanh (Parallax Press, 2016)

Meditation for Relaxation: 60 Meditative Practices to Reduce Stress, Cultivate Calm & Improve Sleep by Adam O'Neill (Althea Press, 2019)

Mindfulness for Beginners: Reclaiming the Present Moment—and Your Life by Jon Kabat-Zinn (Sounds True, 2016)

The Mindfulness Journal for Anxiety: Daily Prompts and Practices to Find Peace by Tanya J. Peterson, MS, NCC (Althea Press, 2018)

The Mindfulness Workbook for Anxiety: The 8-Week Solution to Help You Manage Anxiety, Worry & Stress by Tanya J. Peterson, MS, NCC (Althea Press, 2018)

Articles

Anxiety Self-Help Articles by Tanya Peterson: https://www.healthyplace.com/self-help/anxiety/anxiety-self-help-articles

"Beyond Worry: How Psychologists Help with Anxiety Disorders" by The American Psychological Association: https://www.apa.org/helpcenter/anxiety

"How to Meditate Deeply & Effectively—a Step by Step Guide" by Enlightenment Portal: https://enlightenmentportal.com/meditation/how-to-meditate-deeply

"Using Mindfulness for Anxiety: Here's How" by Tanya J. Peterson: https://www.healthyplace.com/self-help/anxiety/using-mindfulness-for-anxiety-here-s-how

"How to Reduce Workplace Stress and Anxiety: Tips for Employees and Management" by Christian Hahn: https://www.anxiety.org/employers-employees-can-manage-workplace-anxiety-and-improve-job-performance

Websites

The following websites provide trustworthy and useful information about anxiety.

Anxiety and Depression Association of America (ADAA): https://www.adaa.org

Anxiety-Schmanxiety Blog: https://www.healthyplace.com/blogs/anxiety-schmanxiety

Calm Clinic: https://www.calmclinic.com

HealthyPlace Mental Health Support, Resources & Information: https://www.healthyplace.com

On these websites, you'll discover information about anxiety and tools for reducing anxiety and living well with it.

Anxiety.org: https://www.anxiety.org

Mindful: https://www.mindful.org

Smart Goals Guide: https://www.smart-goals-guide.com

Social Anxiety Association: https://socialphobia.org

VIA (Values in Action) Institute on Character: https://www.viacharacter.org

REFERENCES

Introduction

National Institute of Mental Health. "Prevalence of Any Anxiety Disorder among Adults." 2017. https://www.nimh.nih.gov/health /statistics/any-anxiety-disorder.shtml.

Newman, Tim. "Anxiety in the West: Is It on the Rise?" *Medical News Today*. September 5, 2018. https://www.medicalnewstoday .com/articles/322877.php.

World Health Organization. "Depression and Other Common Mental Disorders: Global Health Estimates." 2017. https://apps .who.int/iris/bitstream/handle/10665/254610/WHO-MSD-MER -2017.2-eng.pdf.

Chapter One

American Psychiatric Association. *Diagnostic and Statistical Manual of Mental Disorders*. 5th ed. Arlington, VA: American Psychiatric Publishing, 2013.

Anxiety and Depression Association of America. "Am I Having a Panic Attack or a Heart Attack?" Accessed July 2019. https:// adaa.org/living-with-anxiety/ask-and-learn/ask-expert/how -can-i-tell-if-i'm-having-panic-attack-or-heart-atta.

Godin, Seth. *Poke the Box: When Was the Last Time You Did Something for the First Time?* New York: Portfolio, 2015.

Chapter Two

Burns, David D. *The Feeling Good Handbook.* New York: Plume, 1999.

Marano, Hara E. "Our Brain's Negative Bias." *Psychology Today.* June 9, 2016. https://www.psychologytoday.com/us/articles /200306/our-brains-negative-bias.

Peterson, Tanya J. "Work around the Negativity Bias to Ease Anxiety." *HealthyPlace Anxiety-Schmanxiety* (blog). 2017. https:// www.healthyplace.com/blogs/anxiety-schmanxiety/2017/06 /we-have-a-negativity-bias-that-causes-anxiety.

Raghunathan, Raj. "How Negative Is Your 'Mental Chatter'?" *Psychology Today.* October 10, 2013. https://www.psychologytoday .com/us/blog/sapient-nature/201310/how-negative-is-your -mental-chatter.

Sasson, Remez. "How Many Thoughts Does Your Mind Think in One Hour?" *Success Consciousness.* Accessed July 2019. https:// www.successconsciousness.com/blog/inner-peace/how-many -thoughts-does-your-mind-think-in-one-hour.

Tolle, Eckhart. *A New Earth: Awakening to Your Life's Purpose.* New York: Penguin, 2008.

Chapter Three

Beck, Aaron T. "Negative Core Beliefs in CBT." Beck Cognitive Behavior Therapy Institute. January 8, 2014. https://beckinstitute.org/negative-core-beliefs-in-cbt.

Bloch, D. "Healing Your Negative Core Beliefs." December 18, 2013. https://www.youtube.com/watch?v=xIWmG45mYsk.

Cascio, Christopher, et al. "Self-Affirmation Activates Brain Systems Associated with Self-Related Processing and Reward and Is Reinforced by Future Orientation." *Social Cognitive and Affective Neuroscience* 11, no. 4 (April 2016). doi:10.1093/scan/nsv136.

Holland, Emily. "Retrain Your Brain: How to Reverse Negative Thinking Patterns." The Chopra Center. Accessed July 2019. https://chopra.com/articles/retrain-your-brain-how-to-reverse-negative-thinking-patterns.

Chapter Four

Csikszentmihalyi, Mihaly. *Flow: The Psychology of Optimal Experience.* New York: Harper Perennial Modern Classics, 2008.

Kabat-Zinn, Jon. *Full Catastrophe Living: Using the Wisdom of Your Body and Mind to Face Stress, Pain, and Illness.* Revised ed. New York: Bantam, 2013.

Kabat-Zinn, Jon. *Wherever You Go, There You Are: Mindfulness Meditation in Everyday Life.* New York: Hachette Books, 2005.

Littrell, Jill. "The Mind-Body Connection: Not Just a Theory Anymore." *Social Work in Health Care* 46, no.4 (February 2008). doi:10.1300/J010v46n04_02.

Peterson, Tanya J. "When Mindfulness Doesn't Calm Anxiety." HealthyPlace. April 30, 2014. https://www.healthyplace .com/blogs/anxiety-schmanxiety/2014/05/when-mindfulness -doesnt-calm-anxiety.

Tolle, Eckhart. *Oneness with All Life: Inspirational Selections from A New Earth.* New York: Penguin Books, 2009.

Chapter Five

Jepsen, Matthew. "Ball in a Pool." In *The Big Book of ACT Metaphors.* Jill A. Stoddard & Niloofar Afari, eds. Oakland, CA: New Harbinger Publications, 2014.

Jepsen, Matthew. "Thought/Emotional Avoidance and Acceptance: Ball in a Pool." Association for Contextual Behavioral Science. Accessed July 2019. https://contextualscience.org /thoughtemotional_avoidance_and_acceptance_ball_in.

Kaplan, Johanna S., and David F. Tolin. "Exposure Therapy for Anxiety Disorders." *Psychiatric Times* 28, no. 9 (September 6, 2011). https://www.psychiatrictimes.com/anxiety/exposure-therapy -anxiety-disorders.

Chapter Six

Anxiety and Depression Association of America. "Exercise for Stress and Anxiety." Accessed August 4, 2019. https://adaa.org /living-with-anxiety/managing-anxiety/exercise-stress-and -anxiety.

Hanh, Thich Nhat. *Peace Is Every Step: The Path of Mindfulness in Everyday Life.* New York: Bantam, 1992.

Naidoo, Uma. "Nutritional Strategies to Ease Anxiety." *Harvard Health Blog.* April 13, 2016. https://www.health.harvard.edu/blog /nutritional-strategies-to-ease-anxiety-201604139441.

Peterson, Tanya J. "List of Foods that Help and Hurt Anxiety." HealthyPlace. 2017. https://www.healthyplace.com/self-help /anxiety/list-of-foods-that-help-and-hurt-anxiety.

Peterson, Tanya J. "Relaxation Techniques for Anxiety: How to Relax Your Mind." HealthyPlace. 2017. https://www.healthyplace .com/self-help/anxiety/relaxation-techniques-for-anxiety-how -to-relax-your-mind.

Peterson, Tanya J. "Yoga for Anxiety Is Very Helpful." Healthy-Place. 2017. https://www.healthyplace.com/self-help/anxiety /yoga-for-anxiety-is-very-helpful.

National Institute of Neurological Disorders and Stroke. "Brain Basics: Understanding Sleep." Accessed August 7, 2019. https:// www.ninds.nih.gov/Disorders/Patient-Caregiver-Education /Understanding-Sleep.

General

Chopra, Deepak, and Rudolph E. Tanzi. *The Healing Self.* New York: Harmony Books, 2018.

Chopra, Deepak, and Rudolph E. Tanzi. *Super Genes.* New York: Harmony Books, 2015.

Daitch, Carolyn. *Anxiety Disorders: The Go-to Guide for Clients and Therapists.* New York: W.W. Norton & Company, 2011.

Day, Susan. *Theory and Design in Counseling and Psychotherapy.* Boston: Lahaska Press, 2004.

Seligman, Linda. *Theories of Counseling and Psychotherapy: Systems, Strategies, and Skills.* 2nd ed. Upper Saddle River, NJ: Pearson Education, 2006.

ABOUT THE AUTHOR

Tanya J. Peterson, MS, NCC, is loving life's rollercoaster (but hates actual rollercoasters). She's lived with anxiety, brain injury, and autoimmune disorders. Despite these, she has created genuine happiness and well-being. How? By learning to both reduce her symptoms and develop tools for living well despite any anxiety and stresses that pop up. Formerly a teacher and counselor, Tanya writes and speaks to empower people to overcome anxiety and other obstacles, create a quality life, and thrive. She writes extensively for HealthyPlace.com, including the weekly *Anxiety-Schmanxiety* blog. Her other books include *Break Free: Acceptance and Commitment Therapy in 3 Steps*, *The Mindfulness Workbook for Anxiety*, and *The Mindfulness Journal for Anxiety*.

CPSIA information can be obtained
at www.ICGtesting.com
Printed in the USA
JSHW060314220922
30813JS00008B/219